FINANCIAL FREEDOM IN THE FUTURE

BRANDON MAX

ISBN: 978-1-4834-8261-3 (sc)
ISBN: 978-1-4834-8262-0 (hc)
ISBN: 978-1-4834-8260-6 (e)

Lulu Publishing Services rev. date: 09/05/2018

Thanks to all my family and friends who gave me the courage and inspiration to write this book. I hope this book helps other people to seek out their own true potential and dreams and to believe in themselves.

Contents

1   Foreword by Joe Citrano Jr. ix

2   Financial Freedom in the Future 1

3   Living in bad conditions 2

4   Working in the Factory...3

5   Joe doesn't take a chance 5

6   The Insurance Man..6

7   Time to Focus 7

8   How can I save money?..7

9   How can I afford to save?..8

10   The Insurance man / Advisor 10

11   First time - First lesson in renting out property 11

12   A real Home..14

13   Peaks and Valleys 15

14   Feeling Good Again 17

15   Mr. Mike with some advice 18

16   Sales people and good credit...................................18

17   Helping out a friend...19

18   How to build your credit 20

19   Laddering Real Estate 21

20   Lawyers that love landlords....................................22

21   Real Estate – Problems you run into while renting out your properties..22

22   Things to remember in real estate 23

23   Dirt lots for sale..25

24   Time to build 26

25   Trouble in Paradise 28

26   Lawyer time...30

27   Starting over again..30

28   Contractor building home 32

29	The appraiser	33
30	Time to buy	34
31	The inspection	36
32	Trouble with tenants	37
33	Landlord turns in to Negotiator	40
34	Central air out of commission	41
35	Flip and move on	42
36	Economy turns bad	43
37	Don't judge a book buy its cover	45
38	Land for sale	47
39	The plan (investment)	48
40	How you can allocate your money in Retirement	50
41	How to diversify your retirement money	52
42	Joe's retirement chart	53
43	Rainy Days and Monies	54
44	Tip Bits	56
45	Rope of Life	60
46	Glossary	61
47	The Message	63
48	Joe's spreadsheet	64
49	Joe's lease contract (Residential)	65
50	Joe's lease contract (Commercial)	70
51	Notes	95
52	Notes	96
53	Notes	97
54	Notes	98
55	Notes	99

Financial Freedom in the Future

This story tells about me a blue-collar worker named Joe. I take you through my financial world. I tell you all about my struggles making a living in a working factory, warehouse and security jobs while still trying to invest in buying and selling real estate, stocks and promissory notes. As i go through the peaks and valleys of the financial world you learn the lessons that i learned so you can avoid the same mistakes. I give you a lease that I use on my own properties so you can copy it and make your own changes for your own properties. **Financial Freedom in the Future** is set up so you can have income in the future when you get ready to retire. **Financial Freedom in the Future** beginning now so you can have a retirement income later. I give you tip bits to help give you encouragement and strength so you can do all these things that I did even bigger and better. You don't have to reinvent the wheel on real estate and investments, it's already here. I show you how to use different buckets for your income. Get out of the rut and start your clear path to **Financial Freedom in the Future**.

Joe Citrano Jr.

Financial Freedom in the Future

Financial Freedom in the Future means later on in life. You will have the freedom to do what you want to do when you want to do it. The system that I recommend in this book tells the story and hopefully a plan of action. **Financial Freedom in the Future** for you and your family. Instead of working all your life with nothing to show for it. Start working for your financial freedom in the future now. This book will tell you how to get started. I learned that in order to get started to have Financial Freedom in the Future, you will need a plan of action. Start with an outline and in it have step #1, step #2, step #3.

Hi, my name is Joe and I'm gone to tell you how to seek Financial Freedom in the Future. I'm not a professional advisor or even pretend to be one. I have worked a blue-collar job all my life. This story, I hope, will give people all over the inspiration that if Joe can do it, I can do it better. The story I write about is for the people who work hard every day, for a little bit of money, they earn after the Vultures get done taking what they can get out of their pay check. Slavery in America is still here. The only difference is we get paid for our labor although not always what it is worth. Americans are not afraid of hard work. In this book I tell about how I go through in peaks and valleys of life. **Financial Freedom in the Future** tells of how we sometimes have to crawl before we walk. It's not how much money we make it's what we do with it that counts. Have faith in God and yourself. Investments in real estate, stocks and any other things can be fun, but it can also be ugly. So you will learn how I faced the good and the bad in investments.

Living in bad conditions

I lived in a small town I called the Boondocks. I didn't know anything outside the world I lived in. I had a high school diploma; people around me all smoked cigarettes and drank their beer and not worrying about the future. They always said don't worry about an education you can always get a job working in the factories. After a few years working as a shoe salesman I quit that job. I started work in a factory where they built cars on one side of the plant and pickup trucks on the other side. Before I tell you about my first day at the factory let me tell you about my living conditions. My living condition, were not that good. I lived on the first floor of this three story rowhome in a one bedroom apartment with just a kitchen and bath and no living room. This three story rowhome had paint peeling off the walls and roaches running wild. The heat for the first floor was two pot belly Ben Franklin stoves, one in the kitchen and one in the bedroom. Each morning you had to put wood or coal in the stoves to get heat. In the summer you would have a metal fan that blew hot air. Everyday I went to the neighborhood tavern we all called the Fish house, every day after work I would get my six pack of beer and two packs of cigarettes and I would go home smoke my cigarettes and drink my beer and get ready for work the next day.

Everyday would go back to a smelly dirty work place. People all around me were all doing the same thing. I didn't have a car so I would have to catch two buses to work. Some days I had to walk to or from work because the buses were late or stopped running at a certain time.

Working in the Factory

I started my first factory job in an assembly plant that built both cars and trucks all in one plant. The north side of the plant built pick-up trucks, cross the train tracks on the south side they built the cars. Having never worked in a large factory before it was scary in the beginning. My first day I had a hard time keeping up with the trucks coming down the assembly line. I was ready to quit my first day on the job. I noticed five guys standing around my area laughing and watching me struggling to keep up with the moving assembly line. Some of the guys were saying that I wasn't gone to last the night out ha, ha, ha. So, there I was saying to myself, I'm not gone to let those guys win. One older gentleman came over to me and said sit down son and let me show you how it's really done. The older gentleman who I called Mr. Gray showed me how to do the job in steps. (procedures). I started Step one, step two, step three. After following the steps over and over again I learned how to do the job the right way. ha, ha, ha. Because of the nice people like Mr. Gray, who went out his way to help me, I would like to help people get started in the same manner with their financial freedom in the future. Start a procedure of investing and keep repeating it over and over again. Later on, you can become independent and help someone else do the same procedure.

One day a friend from the factory I worked with ask me to take a ride. He took me out to see how other people really live. What I seen was amazing. I saw single family homes with two car garages and manicured lawns. No drunks hanging on the street corners, no trash in the streets. This was really great I said to my friend Mark. How can I get out of my world and into this one? Mark told me that I had to do a plan of action. He said action is just a word and it's up to me to make it happen. Working in the factory I met some good people and some bad ones.

Joe doesn't take a chance

I didn't take a chance and I said to myself, I should have and would have but I was afraid. One day a friend named George came to me and ask me to go into a partnership with him. He told me about an old burnt out commercial building for sale. The building he was talking to me about was in the area where I lived. The place where I grew up I always called the Boondocks because nothing was really around us except the packing houses, factories, breweries, and taverns on almost every corner. The waterfront had tug boats and broken piers with wharf rats as big as cats. I told George that this place has nothing around us to make me want to do this investment. We had no restaurants, grocery stores, shopping centers nothing here to attract people and businesses to come here. George explained to me that what you call the Boondocks is an up and coming neighbor called Canton. George said that we could each put in $25,000 for a total of $50,000 and we could double or triple our money. One of my biggest mistakes I ever made was telling George no and I turned the deal down. To my surprise 10 years later what George said to me came true. The place I called the Boondocks became well known as Canton. The old factories, packing houses, warehouses were all replaced with shopping centers, restaurants, new office buildings, condos, new townhouses and boat marinas with boat slips. The waterfront had new piers and a walkway that stretched all around the waterfront from the eastside to the southside of town. Instead of watching tug boats in the harbor you could see all types of recreational boats that glided across the water. People wanted to be on the water or looking at it, that turned this into a great place to work and shop. The community I grew up in had all changed for the better. George was a smart businessman who had vision to look at things to come in the future. My hope is to give you the same vision George gave me. Don't be afraid to take some chances in life. Say to yourself I can do it. Stay away from the negative people and stay with the positive ones.

The Insurance Man

One day a friend of mine named Dave introduced me to his insurance man / advisor. The insurance man sold me some life insurance ; put me into a mutual fund and had me dollar cost average into it each month. Example. $100.00 deposited into the mutual fund every month systematically. The insurance man told me to save my money for a down payment on a house instead of renting. He told me to start a bucket list and to write down the things I wanted in it. He said in time you will achieve all your golds on your bucket list if you stay focused on it. Start by getting rid of the things you don't need and focus on the things you do need.

Time to Focus

How I could save money to invest for the future. I thought about how I could stop unnecessary spending. I Started to say to myself is it a want or is it a need. Need is now, want is later. So, it was up to me to stop my unnecessary spending and focus on my own priorities which was my financial freedom in the future.

I stopped drinking, smoking and spending money on unnecessary things. I sat down and made a list and decided to take a plan of action.

How can I save money?

1. Fast food (lunch) $6.00 a day=$30.00 week = $120.00 month $1,440.00 year
2. Coffee (morning) $5.00 a day=$25.00 week = $100.00 month $1,200.00 year
3. transportation $4.00 a day=$20.00 week = $80.00 month $960.00 year
4. new clothes ----------------------------- = $100.00 month $1,200.00 year
5. internet & phone $5.00 a day=$25.00 week = $100.00 month $1,200.00 year
6. cigarettes $5.00 a day= $25.00 week = $100.00 month $1,200.00 year

7. alcohol $5.00 a day= $25.00 week = $100.00 month $1,200.00 year
8. entertainment ------------- $100.00 week = $400.00 month $4,800.00 year

Money spent for a whole year total $250.00 week = $1,000.00 month $12,000.00 year

I put just a little money each month in an IRA Roth and IRA Traditional. I was on my way to Financial Freedom in the Freedom.

How can I afford to save?

I found $6,000.00 that I could save just by cutting cost in my budget. This money could go into investments for my retirement, or buy my first home.

$6,000.00 year X 5 years = $30,000.00

$6,000.00 year X 10 years = $60,000.00

$6,000.00 year X 15 years = $90,000.00

$6,000.00 year X 20 years = $120,000.00

All figures are not showing how much more your money would grow. If you included the interest, dividends or capital gains over the years of investing.

Your bucket list can contain the following for your Financial Freedom in the Future.

IRA Roth   Individual Retirement Account

IRA Traditional   Individual Retirement Account

Mutual Funds, ETF'S, index Funds

Stocks - large cap, mid cap, small cap, international

Bonds - corporate, government, international

Real estate - commercial, residential

Cd's - certificates of deposit

Promissory notes - a financial and debt instrument in which one party agrees to pay the other party a determinate sum of money in a certain time frame.

Start your own business - LLC. Limited Liability Company

Sole proprietor ship - unincorporated business that is owned by an individual

I could do all this and make it happen with just a plan of action.

The Insurance man / Advisor

The insurance man / advisor told me to stay in my run-down apartment for a few more years. He told me to invest and save my money. So, I stayed in my run-down apartment with my black and white television and the bums sleeping in the hallway by the door at night. The insurance man told me to buy a 3 bedroom townhouse and to rent it out for two years. He told me to go out and buy new furniture. He told me to tell the store to put it on an installment plan and don't deliver it until they get my ok. This will help build up my credit and in two years it will be paid. It will also help me save money on storage and delivery charges. I bought the 3 bedroom townhouse and the new furniture. I started paying on furniture that I really didn't have yet and a townhouse that I didn't live in. I paid monthly payments into a mutual fund that I knew nothing about. I had a friend who ask me if he could rent out my townhouse to he and his family. He promised to take good care of it so I said ok. The new tenant moved in to my townhouse giving me his word and not signing any lease agreement. Later this would be a costly mistake on my part. Still setting golds I decided to call a contractor in to add new windows and doors to the townhouse while the tenants were living in the house.

After three years of the Insurance man / advisor taking my money and putting it into his own company mutual fund and collecting commissions from his company and me. I decided that I would read up on different mutual funds. I found out about other mutual fund companies that were lower cost commission brokers that charged lower fee's than what I was paying. I really learned some good lessons in the world of finance from the insurance man. My thanks to the insurance man for pointing me in the right direction when at that time of my life I didn't know what direction I was going in. Thank God that I was able to stay focused and follow my financial freedom in the future for my retirement. I learned that I paid a higher price in the beginning but that was well worth the education it taught me. The insurance man / advisor wasn't a bad guy.

First time - First lesson in renting out property

I rented my first investment property out. A nice little 3 bedroom townhouse that I rented out to a friend. He promised me that he would take good care of my investment and always pay the rent on time. I trusted him at his word and didn't draw up any agreement or take a security deposit. Well little did I know about how some tenants really are. First lesson in real estate or any other business transaction is to get contract in writing. Get the contract written up by your lawyer so it has all your wants and needs in it. Once you sign on the dotted line it becomes a legal agreement between you and the other party. First lesson in real estate is don't trust anybody but yourself to make that final decision. You will get what I call a gut feeling and sometimes you will have to go with that certain gut feeling. Six months later my so-called friend moved out of my house in the middle of the night without paying his rent. I went over to look at the house after I found out that they have left. What I found was they had damaged the house and it was a wreck in need of a lot of repairs. The kids had over flowed the upstairs tub which caused water to flow down downstairs and through the living room ceiling. Kids broke the fan to the central air unit by putting sticks in it trying to stop the fan. Even the dog got into wrecking the house by chewing up the wooden stair case. My so-called friend didn't even give me a notice that he was leaving.

There I was with my first rental property with no rent and no security deposit. Time for plan of action. I called Police and they said that I didn't have a leg to stand on because I didn't have anything in writing such as a lease agreement. The Police Officer said off the record. If you get a tenant that never pays you the rent on time or always falls way behind in rent and they act like they don't care.

He told me there is a way to get rid of your tenant. He explained to me if you make your tenants comfortable they will stay, if you make them uncomfortable they will leave. Make your tenants uncomfortable. I asked him how can I do that without breaking the law. He explained off the record. Make sure in your lease agreement that the landlord has the right to come to the house to make repairs. One day go to the house where the tenants live and tell them you are coming to make some repairs. The first thing you are going to do is take the front and back doors off. Put the doors in your truck and drive away. Don't come back until later on that night. The tenants will have to stay home all day in the house to watch the things in the house so nothing gets stolen. They know for a fact that if they don't stay home and watch their belonging they may come home to an empty house. Later when the tenants take you to court show the judge the lease agreement. The lease agreement says that the landlord has the right to make repairs on his property that the tenants are renting. I had to think of my own plan of action. I took all the tenants mail that was coming to the rental house and put it in a brown paper bag. Later I got a phone call from the tenant that moved out. He said " Joe could I have my mail that was sent to your house". I said" could I have my rent money that you forgot to pay me". I told him that I wasn't going to keep his mail. But, if I didn't receive my rent money, I was gone to put return to sender on every letter and take it all to the post office. He said please don't do that I will give you your rent money. Later that week I had my rent money in cash and he had his mail. Plan of action. I called a realtor to find me a tenant and a contractor to fix the house back up. In a month, had a new tenant with all my wants and needs in the lease agreement.

A real Home

Two years later I went out and bought a new car. My reasoning for buying a new car was I didn't want to buy someone else's problems. I know people say that a new car is not a good investment. My reason for doing this was that you get a warranty if something does go wrong with it. The furniture that I was paying on for two years was paid. I called the furniture store and set up a date for delivery. I went to the post office to mail a certified letter informing the tenants that I would not be renewing their lease. At last I moved into a real home leaving everything else behind me only taking my clothes with me. I was really glad to have a real home with 3 bedrooms and two baths and a living room. Here I was a single guy with a 3 bedroom house so I knew I had to come up with a plan of action to help my cash flow. I decided that I would rent out the two other bedrooms for income. I had my new tenants pay me weekly instead of monthly. In case they didn't pay me, I could get them out by the end of the month and not waste a whole month without rent. By me charging weekly instead of monthly you get a little bit more money because you have more weeks in some months than others.

Peaks and Valleys

For 2 years I enjoyed being in my home. Two years later I got a lay off slip from my job and my parents pasted away all in the same year. I felt lonely and depressed to the point that I didn't hold a steady job down for 5 years. One day I said to myself I have to make a plan of action. I sold my home in the county and moved back into the city where I grew up. The area I called the Boondocks is now called Canton where people want to come to live. It was an upcoming and growing community where the prices of the homes were starting to rise in value. Everybody wanted to be near or by the water. People started putting decks on the roof tops of their rowhomes so they could see the water. I had a plan. My plan was to take this 3 story townhouse building that I bought and convert it into 3 separate apartments. The second and third stories of the apartment building would have their own fireplace and decks that had views of the water. The plan was to gut out the whole building and replace it all with electric, plumbing, central air, heating system and etc. I learned a big lesson in real estate. I was trying to live in it and fix it up at the same time. The 3 story rowhouse with two gutted out floors and me living on the second floor with peeling paint and roaches running wild. Every time I tried to fix something another thing went wrong. What I thought was going to be easy turned out to be a big disappointment. Money was running low and I had no job. This project of mine was a real big letdown. Time to stop feeling sorry for myself and it's time to start another plan of action. I decided to sell this 3 story townhouse. Later on, I would try another project after I have more experience and knowledge. I should have had a better understanding of how much money and time really goes into a project like this. Maybe next time I will have better luck.

I started my next plan of action. I got a job as a temporary worker at a warehouse not far from the 3 story townhouse I was living in. I had to sell my car because the money was running low. To save money I could walk to work or even catch a bus. I called a realtor to sell my 3 story townhouse in Canton. The realtor said that if he could not sell my home in 3 months that he would buy It from me. I signed the contract with the realtor and started looking for another home close to where I was working so I could still walk to work or catch a bus.

I started my plan of action. Two months had pasted and I saw a townhouse for sale that I really liked. It wasn't too far from work so I could walk or catch a bus. I went to the house that was for sale and asked them if I could take a look at the house they were selling. FSBO means for sale by owner. It was a nice little two story townhouse that had just been rehabbed. It had two bedrooms, one and a half baths, club basement and central air. The price they told me I thought was too high . I went back a second time and ask them if they would lower the price down if I would pay all the closing cost. I explained to them that they would still be saving money on the deal. I told them that I would be putting down ten thousand dollars down towards the home. I would be saving money by taking most of the closing cost off my income taxes. Now I went to a mortgage banker who was a good friend of mine named Jerry. Jerry said he would get the paper work started. The banker contacted my full-time employer and got written information on me working for that company showing I had income. I called the realtor who told me he would buy my house if it didn't sell. I sold the three story townhouse with the two gutted out floors as is to the realtor for what I bought it for and walked away from my project.

Feeling Good Again

I moved into my new rehabbed home and started to feel good again. A plan of action. I decided to rent out one of the other bedrooms for extra income money and again my new tenant would be paying me by the week not by the month. I still had a living room and a club basement that I could use for entertaining my friends. The area I lived in was an up and coming community now called Canton. I could go for a walk in the park or take a walk down to the new water front.

Mr. Mike with some advice

Mr. Mike owned a tavern where I used to stop in from time to time see him. One day he said to me Joe when you get married have two bank accounts. I asked him why. Mr. Mike told me to have one bank account in my name and the other bank account in my wife's and my name in a joint account. He told me that down the road if the marriage ever ended you wouldn't be left out in the cold. You would have something to help you get back on your feet again. Mr. Mike said if it does work out later you will have a nice retirement nest egg for you and your wife.

Sales people and good credit

A few years later after settling down in my new rehabbed home. I got married and we had one son, one dog and one cat. Life was good. One day I came home and ask my wife who has that new car parked outside our house. She explained to me that new car was ours. I asked her just how did we get this new car. She said the guy at the dealership said when he ran our credit that we had good credit. So, I pulled out a credit card and put one thousand dollars down on the new car we now have sitting in front of our house. I had to explain to her that he was a salesman and that his job was to make sales. Just because we have good credit you have to still be care full not to ruin it. Plastic credit cards are still a form of real money and that we have to pay them back with interest. Now we not only have to pay on a credit card but also a car loan from the dealership. I told her next time let's talk about it first so I don't come home to any more surprises. We are doing ok as a family paying our bills and taking vacations two times a year.

Helping out a friend

Working in a factory you meet a lot of people and make friends. Tony was a good friend and we worked together for ten years. One day Tony came into work telling me that his wife had left him and his son. Tony said he felt down and out. I told Tony that all he needed was a plan of action." Tony ", I said" here you are in this big house with just you paying all the bills. Take the top part of your house and turn it into an apartment. This will bring you in some extra income to help you pay some of your bills. Tony went ahead and made the upstairs top floor a separate rental apartment. Tony now had some extra money coming in to help him pay some of his bills. Tony asked me if I would help him get more into residential real estate by showing him how to own more properties and renting them out for income. I showed Tony the plan of action. Tony now has five rentals with tenants living upstairs and downstairs in each one of his rentals. Tony used the ladder system by borrowing the equity from one home to buy another home. Tony 's father called me up and said "Thanks Joe. You created a monster. Tony was so depressed after his wife left him and now he's very happy again Thanks again". I told Tony one of the rules in picking out properties you want to buy. Always look in the back yards and alleys before you decide to buy a home for an investment property. The front of the home could look real nice. If the neighborhood around your home is bad you better look before you leap. Try to go see the neighborhood in the evening time that's when you really see if it's good or bad.

How to build your credit

Sometimes people who have no credit have trouble buying a house or even car. I had a friend come to me and ask me if I could help her. She said her credit was bad from mistakes she had made in the past. I told her to apply for a secured credit card from a bank or credit card company. The young lady applied for a secured credit card from her bank putting up five hundred dollars of her own money to secure it. The bank issued her a secured credit card in her own name for five hundred dollars. She went out and bought four hundred dollars worth of things she needed and charged it on her new credit card. Every month she put money towards the bill. One year later she applied for an unsecured credit card and got it. Two years later she applied for a home loan and got it. She said thanks Joe for taking the time to tell me how to make my credit better.

Laddering Real Estate

I told a friend of mine one day if you are renting stop wasting your money. Think about owning your own home. Buy a three bedroom townhouse. Rent two of the extra bedrooms out while you are living in the third bedroom. Think rowhouse first because they are cheaper to buy when you are first starting out. Think about a good location by schools, churches and shopping. Later borrow the equity in the home to buy another home. When you are borrowing from one home to buy another one this is a form of laddering.

Lawyers that love landlords

One day a tenant and his friend got together to sue the landlord. The tenant said his friend fell down the back steps because of a lose wooden step. They sued the landlord and split the settlement money given to them from the insurance company. The tenant and his friend were telling the next store neighbor how they got easy money from the landlord.

Be careful with rental homes or commercial properties that have lead paint, mold, asbestos materials inside or outside of them. Lawyers love landlords with these things in or outside their properties.

Real Estate – Problems you run into while renting out your properties

*Tenants who can't pay the rent.

*Tenants who leave behind bed bugs.

*Tenants who wreck your property.

*Tenants who move out in the middle of the night.

*Tenants who move out knowing that their kids have over flowed the tub.

*Tenants who let their pets destroy your investment property.

*Tenants breaking windows and putting holes in sheet rock.

*Tenants leaving nasty odors in the house after they leave.

*Tenants who invite all their friends over to the house to wash their clothes while you get the water bill.

*Tenants who are put out of your house but come back later with a spare key.

These are a few bit of things you will come across being a landlord. I wanted you to know what you will be getting into from a person who has experienced it.

Things to remember in real estate

* Make sure you have two separate checking accounts. One for your business and one for yourself.

* Make sure you always have money in your business account to pay for the following.

* Taxes, maintenance, insurance, before you withdraw any money for yourself.

* Allow money in the budget for empty rental units until you can get a tenant in them.

* If you go into a business you better have a business plan and some money saved to support you for at least a year because things some times are ruff in the beginning.

* If you sign any agreements make sure it is looked over by your lawyer and it has all your wants and needs in it.

* When you draw up a lease agreement put a clause at the end of the contract turning any money owed to the landlord on the property they leased into a promissory note paid to the landlord in their own names as individuals not as an LLC.

*Go to the properties you own every month to change the air filter in the furnace. While you are there changing the air filter you are looking around for any damage that may have occur since your last visit. Look for water leaks, broken windows, doors, bathrooms, kitchen and etc. anything that may need to be fixed.

* Have all bills to your properties sent to your own address of business. (May want to use P.O. Box)

* Send out invoices in e-mail or letters lettings the tenants know that this bill has been paid by you the owner of the said property and that this invoice is asking for reimbursement for the money you paid out.

The reason for this is if certain bills are not paid liens could be put against your properties and you would not know anything about it until later.

*Make sure all water bills, property taxes, etc. are only in your name or your company name. If the bills are in the tenant's name then that is the tenant's problem not yours. The reason the bills are sent to you the landlord so you will know what bills are being paid at that time.

Dirt lots for sale

One day while walking home from work I saw a sign that was on a dirt lot that read lot for sale. I went home and told my wife about the dirt lot for sale. She asked me what I would do with this dirt lot. I told her that I was thinking about building some commercial retail buildings on it. Because it was in a retail district and later that would give us income for the future. She replied back you can't even swing a hammer how do expect to build commercial retail buildings. How do you suppose to get the money to pay for this hair brain idea? I told her that I have a plan of action. Later that week I called the realtor and asked for information on the lot for sale. The realtor told me that instead of one lot for sale there were really three small lots for sale. He explained that each lot was owned by a different family member. I checked the zoning making sure I could build the type of commercial building I wanted in that area. I had the realtor draw up a contract for only buying the middle lot and I put a clause in it. The clause said if the city doesn't let me build on 100 % percent of the lot my contract for buying the said property would become void. I needed to ask for a variance giving me permission to build on 100% percent of the land without a setback. I asked the city if they could grandfather it in meaning I could build on the lot the same size buildings before the other buildings before me. The realtor asked me why are you just buying the middle lot. I replied if I only buy the middle lot at this time the other two people that own their lots cannot expand and would be forced to sell to me. I talked to the bank and they told me that they would give me a second mortgage on my home. Once the building is built I could get mortgages on it to continue my building the other building. After I bought the middle lot I gave the same offer to the owners of the other two lots. They said I will sell the lots to you because I can't expand with just owning one lot.

Time to build

Plan of action. I got all the people I needed together to get my project started. A realtor to find a tenant before the buildings were built. An architect to draw the plans for inside and outside of the buildings to give to the realtor. The realtor could show the plans to potential clients who may be interested in leasing the buildings. I found a bank that would finance the project from the beginning to the end. The realtor said he knew of a contractor who could do all the buildings and the parking lot from the beginning to the end. Everybody and everything was in place the project started moving on. The realtor found a potential client who signed on to be the first tenant of the building that was being built. The contractor was set up to get his money by taking draws. Taking 1/3 of the money each time he needed money until the project was completed. One day during the construction of the retail buildings I got a phone call. The man on the phone said I would l like to talk to the person having the commercial buildings built in back of my house. I said yes sir how may I help you. He told me that he was getting water in his basement every time it rained and it was due to the construction being done by my buildings. I'm going to sue you for the damage you caused with the water coming into my basement. I replied sir your basement had been getting water in it way before my construction even started. I explained to him that the foundation meaning the rocks and gravel under the cemented alley were all washed away over the years. With you not having a foundation under the cemented alley this was causing the water to flow into your basement every time it rained.

I tore the alley all up and put in a new foundation. I put down a new foundation with new rocks and gravel and I ran new drain lines with PVC piping taken the water out to the street away from your home. You shouldn't be getting any water into your basement after all the construction is completed. The man replied is this the Joe Citrano that rented one of my apartments from me years ago. I said yes, I was the young man who rented one of your slum apartments years ago. He said I'm so proud of you, that you turned out to be a successful young man. By the way he said I'm not gone to sue you. Thanks, I said and never heard from him again.

The first building is up after the city and the community associations approved of it. The first tenant is in the building and rent starts coming in to make the mortgage payments each month. Plan of action. I'm ready to build my second building going through the same process. This time I borrowed against the first building with a second mortgage to get the second building built.

Trouble in Paradise

The same contractor who built the first building is now starting the second building. The contractor took fifty thousand dollars and started working on building the second building. Two months later with the building half way built I got a phone call from the contractor. I asked the contractor has something gone wrong at the job site. He explained to me that he had just declared bankruptcy and that he was an LLC. (limited liability Company). Because he was an LLC. I was out of the fifty thousand dollars that he had taken to start the job. Later on that day, the phone started ringing off the hook. The sub -contractors that the contractor had hired to work on my buildings were not paid for the work they did and they said they wanted their money or else they would be putting a lien on my buildings. Here I was out of fifty thousand dollars, I have a building half way built and sub- contractors who I didn't even know or even hire wanting money that I didn't have. At the same time all this is going on my wife was very upset with the whole situation. My wife was arguing with me saying that she wasn't going to stay and watch us lose everything. She told me that she wanted a divorce because I was about to lose everything and she said I'm not staying on a sinking ship. I told her that a good wife stays with her husband to help in good or bad times. I told My wife that I would straighten this mess out with the sub- contractors and that everything would be all right again. My wife said no I'm leaving and taking our son with me. I told her I would give her whatever she wanted. I told my Wife I know where you stand and it isn't with me, so the dreams I have must be mine alone. Plan of action.

Lawyer time

I called the lawyer and explained to him the problems I was having. We set up a meeting in his office to discuss a way out. Plan of action. The lawyer said we will call all the sub-contractors that the general contractor had not paid; we will offer them all half of the money of what the general contractor owed them in return they will all agree to finish the construction of the building. I went to the bank and explained to them what had happen and got the money to pay everybody their money. Three months later the building was completed and I had new tenants paying me rent so I could pay my mortgage. Remember I told you I had bought three lots. The third lot I turned into a parking lot and charged people for private parking spaces. Buildings and lot all producing income.

Starting over again

I told you that my wife wanted off what she called a sinking ship because of all the trouble with the sub-contractors and me losing fifty thousand dollars to the general contractor. So, while I was dealing with the building issues I was also dealing with my wife and I going through a divorce. After the divorce I had to sell the house and give her the car and pay child support. This was all agreed to in the settlement. So, I rented a rowhouse for the dog and me and my son that I had every other week. I was lucky because I could still walk to work. Remember what Mr. Mike told me about having two saving accounts wow was he ever right. Alter paying a landlord rent money for two years I decided that a new plan of action was needed. I started looking at buying a home. Later after looking around I decided to have a house built from the ground up. I saw a lot for sale by owner in the community paper. I called the number and the man selling the lot said he was a contractor. He said he bought the house next store and sub divided the land into two separate properties. He said he sold the house next store. Now he would like to sell the lot that came with it. The man said I will sell you the lot if you let me build the house that you want on it. I met with the contractor and told him that I wanted a 3 bedroom rancher with 3 bathrooms two upstairs and one down in the ten-foot-high basement. I picked out all the paint colors, ceramic tiles, wooden floors and etc. We signed the contract and I gave him money for a down payment. As he started to work on building my new home, I found a reasonable interest rate on a new home. The mortgage loan from the bank was for thirty years because the payments are always lower than the fifteen years. Later if I had extra money I could always make a double payment to lower the years to pay on my new home.

Contractor building home

During the construction of my home I went to the building site every week end. I took pictures of each stage the construction was in. The general contractor was using sub – contractors to do the work. I made sure the contractor put cement board down before putting the ceramic down. The cement board will give a better support for the ceramic being placed down where water or moisture is most likely in a kitchen or bathroom area. Some contractors are like con artist they tell you what you want to hear but still do what they want to do totally different then what you both agreed on. Some contractors will try to do things the cheap way out just to save them self 's time and money on the job. After nine months the new rancher was completed. I got everything I wanted in it except he didn't put the third bathroom in the basement. I asked him where is the third bathroom that was supposed to be in the basement. He told me that he forgot to put it in but for a little extra charge he could add it. Be careful of what contractors promise you. I should had been more observant during the construction of the home but I was so excited about having the new home built that it skipped my mind. After eight months of living in the rancher the front steps started to separate from the front of the house. I called the contractor who came out to patch and repair the front steps. The contractor told me that under the contract that he didn't have to replace the steps and that I only had a one year warranty on my home. The following year I had a new contractor tear out the front steps and pour a better foundation and build the new front steps.

The appraiser

I needed an appraiser to look at one of my properties I was selling. I asked around the neighborhood. One neighbor suggested his brother who was an appraiser and a real estate investor. I called his brother who said he would do the appraisal. I paid him the money up front for the appraisal. After one month I gave him a call. The appraiser said he wasn't in that type of business anymore and that he wasn't returning my money to me. I called his brother and told him about what his brother the appraiser said to me. He said sorry and that he had no control over what his brother does. I said thanks and moved on. Two months had passed and I got a call from the neighbor who said that he couldn't help me get my money back from his brother the appraiser. Hello how can I help you. The man on the phone said that he had a rental house that needs a tenant. He said I thought that you might know someone that may be looking to rent my townhouse. I told him that I did and gave him the phone number of the person that might be interested in renting his rental house. One year had past and I got a phone call from the neighbor who wanted the name of a person wanting to rent his rental house. I answered the phone hello how can I help you. He said Joe I need your help. The tenants that you recommended to me tore my rental house up and left without paying the water bill and the last month of rent. Could you help me get my money that they owe me? I told him that I was sorry for his lost and that I have no control over what his tenants did. I suggested that he get himself a lawyer and take them to court. I remembered what he told me about him having no control over what his brother the appraiser did. His brother the appraiser who took my money never returning it or even giving me the appraisal I paid for. They always say be careful how you treat people because one day you may need their help one day.

Time to buy

One day I was reading the community paper when I ran across an ad in the paper for a one story commercial building. I called the number and talked to the realtor to set up an appointment to go see what the building looked like. The next day I went to see the building. From the outside of the one story building it looked like needed a new roof and some new windows and a new glass front door. Inside the building looked old with old wooded paneling on the walls with lights in the ceiling that gave off very little lighting. It had a bathroom in the back with two other rooms with junk piled in them. I asked the realtor what the asking price was and she told me that they were asking $135,000 for the building as is. I told her that I would offer them $100,000 as is. The next day I went to the bank and asked to borrow some money to buy another building. The bank agreed to loan me the money to buy the building plus $25,000 extra money to fix it up. The following month we had settlement and now I owned three commercial buildings and a very small parking lot. Now I had to have a plan of action. I called in all the contractors that I needed to rehab the inside and outside of the building from top to bottom. The contractors added new plumbing, electric, roof, central air, gas heating system, two bathrooms, and added new lighting to go with the new sheetrock replacing the old wooden paneling. Now the building was completed and I invited all the Neighbors over to see the new place. The neighbors couldn't believe that building they were standing in was the same dirty building. Now the new rehab building was nice and bright and clean with two restrooms. I called my realtor and we had it rented out the following month. I learned later that I had to share my driveway with my neighbor who had an easement put into the deed years ago. The easement was an agreement in the contract where they had the right of way to use my driveway to get to their property. The lesson I learned was that I should had looked before I leaped.

The inspection

One day while driving around I saw a nice little rancher home for sale. I called the realtor and we went to go see it. The rancher looked really nice from the outside. Inside the rancher was a different story. The inside of the rancher needed some TLC. (tender loving care). The doors to all the clothes closets were all off. The whole house was in need of paint. The heating system was electric heat and I preferred gas heat. Sometimes you can have the utility company ran gas lines in to your home to have the gas hook up allowing you to have cheaper utility bills in the cold months. I was going down stairs to the basement club room and that looked ok. The downstairs had a third full size bathroom in it. Unfortunately, the bathroom consisted of your sink, bathtub, and toilet but nothing was hooked up to the water lines. The realtor said I needed to get a plumber to have everything hooked up because the owners only had the ruffed in part done in the basement. The realtor asked me if I wanted an inspection done on the house before I bought it, I told her yes. When the inspector came he inspected the whole house and told me all the problems he had found wrong with it. The inspection found to have polybutylene pipes all through the house. Polybutylene pipe material was said to become weak and flake from the oxidants in the water supplies such as chlorine. In the 1980's lawsuits were filed complaining the alleged usage of defective material. Lawsuits were filed and settled. The inspection also found aluminum wiring all through the whole house. I prefer copper wiring in any home I buy. I called the realtor and told her about the inspection. I got my deposit back and moved on.

Trouble with tenants

I ran into a problem when a tenant called me and told me that he couldn't pay me the rent. I told him that he still had a whole year left on his lease agreement. I had to come with a plan of action. I told the tenant that I would let him stay for one more year with reduced rent if he would sign a promissory note. I told the tenant I would set up an easy payment plan at three hundred dollars a month for five years. Every month I would get on my computer to see if he deposited three hundred dollars into my account that I set up at his bank so he had no excuses why he couldn't make it to the bank. If the money was late I would send him an invoice charging him a late fee of fifty dollars to be deposited to my account. The following year I had a new tenant in my building plus money coming from the promissory note as income each month.

I ran into a problem when a tenant decided to move out of one of my building in the middle of the night and I was stuck with an empty building and a broken glass front door. I contacted my lawyer who issued a lien on the person that broke his lease agreement. The lawyer said that tenant couldn't open up another business in his own name in any state without settling with me. Plan of action. I contacted contractors to paint and fix whatever was broke so I could have it ready for a new tenant. I put a for lease sign in the window and within two weeks I had a new tenant in my building. One month later I got a phone call. I said hello how may I help you. It was from the man who moved out in the middle of the night and left behind a broken glass front door. He said hi Joe how are you. I was wandering if you could help me. I'm in another state and I can't open up another business because you put a lien out on me. I replied oh yes now I remember you. I'll tell you what I want from you. You pay me half the money you owe me on the lease. I want it in a certified check in one week. If you don't pay me, I will come after you for the whole amount. I received a certified check in the mail that week and I faxed him a letter releasing him of his debt owed to me. I always said half is better than nothing.

One day I got a letter from the city about a violation on one of my buildings. The new tenant put out an electric light sign. The tenant had hooked up the electric sign with extension cords where the wires were running outside the building causing a fire hazard. I called the tenant and told her about the problem. I called an electrician to go down to the property and hook up the electric sign by the city code and to send me the bill. I sent the tenant an invoice bill for the electrician and the violation fine sent to me from the city.

One month on one of my properties I didn't receive any rent. This tenant ran an insurance business from out of one of my buildings. I called the tenant and ask him what the problem was that I haven't received my rent for this month. He explained to me that his business partner and him were not getting along and wanted to dissolve the business they have formed together. I told him that I was in the rental business. I explained to him if you don't pay me the rent money that you owe me I will shut your business down and change those locks so fast your head will spin. After I do all that I will take both of you to court and sue for breach of contract. He said to me you drive a hard bargain. I replied back you are in the insurance business. What happens if a client doesn't pay his or her insurance on their car. He said we will cancel the client's policy. I told him that I was doing the same thing but in a different business. Later I had a talk with the both of them and came up with agreement that all of us liked. I ask them to stay in the building paying me my rent on a month to month basis until I could get someone else to rent my building for a longer lease. I told them in return I will let you out of the lease free and clear. When I found a tenant, they were both gone.

Landlord turns in to Negotiator

I had a tenant who wanted to sell his business. Nobody could agree on the price that he was asking for. He could never make up his mind. First, he would tell them one price than later on change his asking price. People called me and told me they wanted to lease my building with his business in it but they could not agree on a price for his business. I asked them if I negotiated a certain price for them would they go along with it. They said yes. I called the man who was selling his business and negotiated a price for his business. I bought the business from the man and sold it to the people who wanted to buy it from him. I could had sold it for more than what I bought it for but I didn't. I gave the new tenants a five year lease with two months of free rent. The lease had five per cent increases built into it to help me keep up with the cost of rising taxes, insurance and maintenance. The lease also had a clause in it that said in case of defaulting on lease that it automatically turns into a promissory note. I took a chance of losing my money from both ends of the deal. Sometimes in business you just have to try to make things happen. My logic for doing this deal was that I saved money by not having to a pay a realtor a fee for finding me a new tenant. Winter time was just around the corner so I knew I had to get new tenants in my building before the cold weather sets in. When you have vacant property in the winter months this is a bad situation because you must keep the heat on at all times so your pipes don't freeze. Always try to get your tenants in before wintertime so you don't have to pay for the heating bill.

Central air out of commission

One hot summer day I got a call from two of my tenants telling me their central air in my buildings wasn't working. I called the maintenance people to go see what the problem was and for them to fix it. Later I got a call back from the maintenance people telling me what the problem was. The maintenance people told me that both central air units had all the copper torn out of them and they would have to be replaced with new units. I was told that people on drugs look for commercial heat and air units to take out all the copper in them and sell the copper so they would have their money to buy drugs to support their habit. I called both tenants and explain to them why their central air units were not working. The tenants had to get fans to try to keep their customer's comfortable until I could get the new central air units. I had to call several companies that sold commercial heat and air units all in one. After making several calls I finally found one that was able to do the job. The damaged air condition units had to be taken off the roof by a crane and new units had to be put in their place. Because of the hot weather the units were on back order. Two months later new units were installed on the roofs.

Flip and move on

One day a friend of mine came to me and ask me if I would be interested in a proposition. He explained that we would go into a business partnership just on buying this one house. The deal was that I would give him forty per cent while he would come up with the sixty per cent. He would pay for all of the maintenance, property taxes, and insurance when we buy this house. A year later the house would be sold and I would receive back my forty per cent plus any profits made off the sale of the house. One year later I collected my money and moved on.

I bought a small rowhouse and cleaned it up. It needed some tender loving care. The first thing I did was to have the roof repaired. Then, fix the ceilings where the roof must had been leaking water to cause the water stains. After all that you want the house to look and smell good. I painted all the rooms and added some nice carpet and before you know it the house is now a home for someone to live in. I bought the house in the month of June and sold it by the end of August. I had to pay Uncle Sam more money because I sold it in less than a year. The tax man said if I would had held it for one year and a day I would had paid less taxes on the gain I made off of it.

I tried going into a partnership with a family member but we both had different ideas and directions on how we wanted to run the business. Before you get started put all your ideas down on paper. If you do decide to go into business together have a way out in your contract.

Economy turns bad

The years of 2008 and 2009 were very bad years where the economy came crashing down. People all over the country were being laid off from their jobs. A lot of large companies were moving the jobs overseas to other countries. By the companies moving their operations overseas they would be saving on the cost of high labor and high taxes. Twenty-three years of working for the same company were all gone. The company that I worked for, decided to down size and a lot of us got laid off from our jobs. The company's 401k was tied in with the stock market. The stock market was down and so was the money we had in the company stock plan for our retirement. I got laid off never to work for them again. When you loose your job with a retirement plan it's very important that you roll the money over into a qualified retirement account with a brokerage or mutual fund company. To just name two that I like are T. Rowe Price and Vanguard but there are many more to chose from. This means putting your retirement money into an IRA - Individual Retirement Account. If your age is less than 59 1/2 and you take your money out of a retirement like a 401k it will be taxed as ordinary income. You can avoid that by having it rolled over into an IRA qualified plan and you will not be paying any penalties for the roll over. If your age is 59 ½ or older you can take the money out and pay little or no taxes on it. In the IRA Roth account your taxes are paid up front and is tax free when you take it out at age 59 1/2 or older with a traditional IRA you get a tax deduction up front and the money is taxed later when you start to draw it out at age 59 ½ or older. I took all the money that was left in the company retirement plan and rolled it over in to a qualified retirement account at a good mutual fund brokerage company. The stock market was really down so I decided to put all my money into a mutual fund that had all the stock sectors in it that I liked. The stock fund had large cap, mid cap, small cap and international stock in it. Some people I worked with at that time cashed their 401k in and had to pay taxes on it.

Don't judge a book buy its cover

I wanted to buy a condo that was owned by the banks. (short sale) A short sale is when a borrower and lender decide that selling the property below the cost of what is owed to the lender. This is a way the borrower can get out of the contract by defaulting on the loan. I saw this condo in the paper as a short sale and decided to call the realtor and get some details on the condo. Within a week I met with the realtor and told him that I was interested in buying the condo. The realtor looked at me the way I was dressed in my blue jeans and a t-shirt and said to me I don't think you could afford the price they are asking. He explained to me that the asking price for the condo was $275,000 and you are only making $12.00 an hour where you work. He told me that I was wasting his time but I really insisted the realtor write up the contract and start the paper work. The realtor said that the condo had a first and second mortgage on it owed by two different banks. I told him that I would offer the bank that had the first mortgage $190,000 for the condo as is and they can let the second bank to take the bigger lost off their books. That week I called my lender and they started doing the paper work for the financing of the condo. I told the lender what the realtor said about how he thought that I couldn't afford to buy the condo. The lender told me not to let the realtor know how much money I was putting down on the condo. A month went by and I called the realtor and asked to see the condo so I could take pictures and measurements and again the realtor had an attitude about showing the condo to me but he did. The banks who owned the condo said that they were in the banking business not the real estate business. The bank decided to sell me the condo for the $190,000. The day of the settlement the realtor and my lender along with the bank who owned the condo all sat down all together to make the deal. I wrote the check out for $100,000 down on the purchase of the condo. The realtor who told me that he thought that I couldn't afford to buy the condo almost fell out of his chair. Mr. Joe said the realtor if I could help you sell your rancher home you have I would be glad to help you do that. I thought to myself, I wouldn't let you sell my dog house because of your attitude towards me in the beginning. Two weeks later I gave the rancher home to another realtor to sell and it sold two weeks l. The lesson is some people are flashy dressers and love to show off then you have some people who are just plain down to earth who don't dress flashy. Some people are very frugal in the way they live their lives. The point that I'm trying to get across is for you to just respect all people because you never know if that person can help you or hurt you in your everyday life. This is why I'm telling you never judge a book by its cover.

Land for sale

I worked in a warehouse where I met Bob. He told me about his father and him wanting to sell land they owned in West Virginia. He said he had two lots for sale with two acres on each lot. Bob was telling me that he and his Father owed two years of property taxes on the 4 acres they own. He said they were thinking about letting the state have it because they couldn't afford to pay the state property taxes. He tried to sell it but could never get a buyer for it. I told Bob that I would give his father and him two thousand dollars each for the land plus pay all the property taxes, lawyer fee's, and all the closing cost at settlement. Bob and his father both agreed. I called a lawyer in West Virginia and he told me that he could handle the settlement of the property. The lawyer charged me two thousand dollars for the whole deal. People said I was crazy for buying land sight unseen. I went down to see the property I bought sight unseen. While I was at the property I had neighbors ask me what I was doing on private property. I told them that I had just bought the property and I wanted to see what I bought. One of the neighbors said he wanted to buy it on a tax lien but someone beat him to it . I told him that was me. Four years later I sold the land for fourteen thousand dollars. The realtor in West Virginia charged me $2,500 in commissions. The state of West Virginia charged me 2.5 income tax on the sale. Remember one thing in business all that is just a tax deduction off the money I made.

The plan (investment)

The plan works in a good or bad economy. When one or two of the buckets are down you won't lose all your money because you are diversified in other investments. The investment plan will pay out all taxes, insurance, maintenance and all liabilities that are set up in the plan. The plan holds buckets and each bucket holds an investment in it. The investments in the plan may contain the following investments. Investments being in real estate, stocks, bonds, certificates of deposits, money markets, IRA'S Roth and Traditional. After all the liabilities are paid out in each investment 20% of profit will go back in to the investment buckets while the rest will go in your bank account for your retirement income. The plan works well if you draw out 4% a month out of each investment bucket you have set up. You may not have to use all the buckets you have all at one time it all depends on how much income you want coming in to you at that time for your retirement.

Liabilities	Real Estate	Bonds	Stocks
Taxes insurance	liabilities	Commercial	individual stocks
maintenance	Insurance	Government	Mutual funds
	Taxes	Municipal	Index funds
	Maintenance	International	International funds
		Promissory notes	ETF's

Rents, interest, dividends and your Social Security check all go in to your retirement money account for your income that you are receiving each and every month.

I like the following investments. Stock mutual funds in large cap, mid cap, small cap, international, index funds and ETF 's. individual stocks, I also like bonds in a mutual fund in Government, Corporate, Municipal and International funds. Real estate commercial and residential investments can be in a REIT or held by you as a landlord. The reason that you are so diversified is to help you in good times and bad times.

Dollar cost averaging – investing the same amount of money each and every month.

Example laddering

CD'S – certificate of deposit

1 year 1%

2 years 3%

3 years 4%

Repeat the same process every year. You can draw money out of your first cd while your other money is drawing interest until you need it.

Laddering houses – every 5 years

Buy one house then wait until the equity builds up into it. Than borrow the equity out of house #1 to buy house #2. Now you are gone to move into house #2 and rent out house #1 and wait until you build up equity in house #2. Now borrow against the equity in house #2 to buy house #3. Move into house #3 and rent out houses #1 and #2. You are going to repeat the same process as you did in one and two and three except instead of buying house #4 you are to take the equity that's built up in house #3 and put it into a IRA Roth or IRA Traditional mutual fund, ETF, or index fund for your retirement. Think. By you following the procedures that I set up you will be on your way to Financial Freedom in the Future.

How you can allocate your money in Retirement

10% Cash	blue
15% Cd's Certificate of deposit	orange
15% Social Security	gray
15% Real Estate	yellow
15% Bonds Govt. Int'l, Corporate	light blue
15% IRA Traditional account	green
15% IRA Roth account	dark blue

This gives you 7 buckets you can pull from. Taken out only 4% each month from each bucket. This will give you income for the rest of your retirement. Get other people started the same way so they also can have Financial Freedom in the Future.

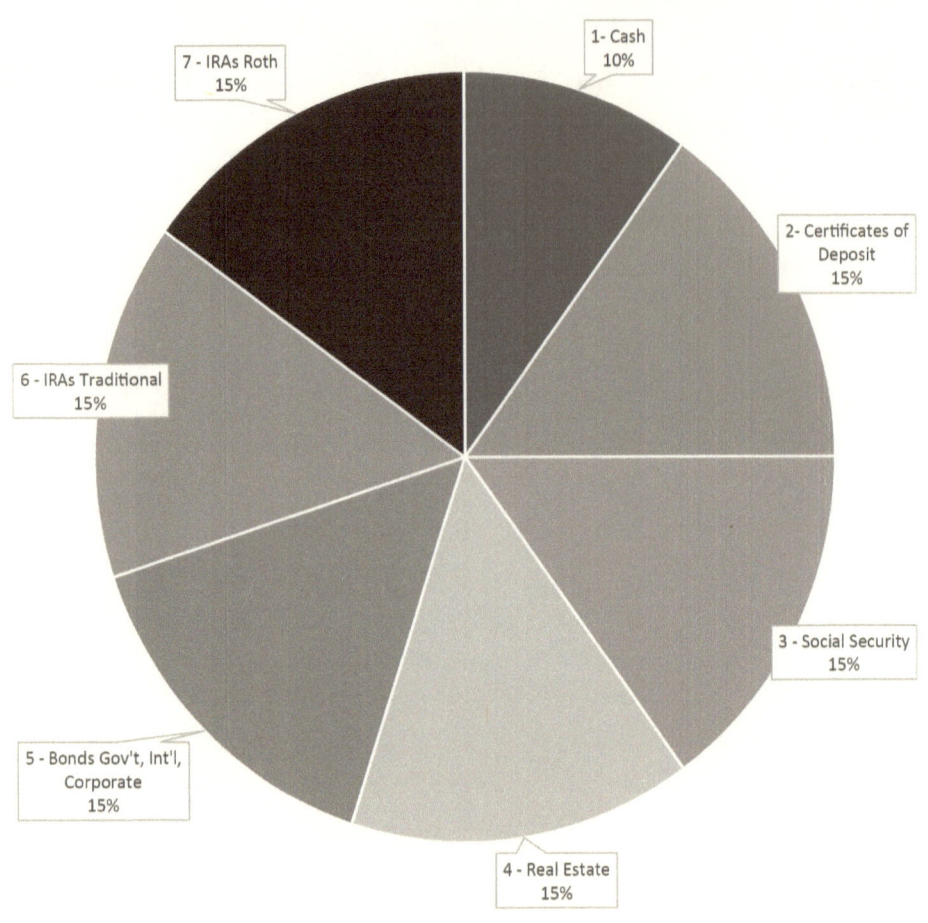

HOW TO DIVERSIFY YOUR RETIREMENT MONEY

7 - IRAs Roth
15%

1- Cash
10%

2- Certificates of
Deposit
15%

6 - IRAs Traditional
15%

3 - Social Security
15%

5 - Bonds Gov't, Int'l,
Corporate
15%

4 - Real Estate
15%

- ■ 1- Cash
- ■ 2- Certificates of Deposit
- ■ 3 - Social Security
- ■ 4 - Real Estate
- ■ 5 - Bonds Gov't, Int'l, Corporate
- ■ 6 - IRAs Traditional
- ■ 7 - IRAs Roth

JOE'S RETIREMENT CHART

TRP ROTH IRA	TRP REG IRA	TRP NON IRA	VANGUARD	REAL ESTATE	REAL ESTATE	REAL ESTATE	REAL ESTATE	SAVINGS	EMERGENCY FUND	SOCIAL SECURITY	NOTES:
											TRY ONLY TO TAKE OUT 4 % OF
											EACH BUCKET EACH YEAR
										• TAKE OUT
										- DON'T TOUCH
										? MAY BE
-	-	-	-	•	•	•	•	•	?	-	AGES 62 - 65
-	-	-	-	•	•	•	•	•	?	•	AGES 66 - 70
?	•	•	•	•	•	•	•	•	?	•	AGES 71 - 75
?	•	•	•	•	•	•	•	•	?	•	AGES 76- 80
?	•	•	•	•	•	•	•	•	?	•	AGES 81 - 87
?	•	•	•	•	•	•	•	•	?	•	AGES 88 - 92
?	•	•	•	•	•	•	•	•	?	•	AGES 93 - 96
?	•	•	•	•	•	•	•	•	?	•	AGES 97 - 100

Rainy Days and Monies

Investing your money is very important for rainy days and for your retirement. Start by paying yourself first. Start setting goals for yourself and tell yourself you can do it. When you start seeking your goals have your plans written down. Have your plans marked with the letters plan A, plan B, plan C. If one plan A doesn't work be prepared to change move on to the next plan. When a person is young they at a great advantage because time means a lot. Investing in mutual funds or ETF's for the future may not cost a lot For a few dollars a month anyone can save. By dollar cost averaging that is money saved and put into a saving account, money market account, mutual fund or ETF the same time each and every week or month all the time. Young people in their twenties should start investing as soon as they can because life goes by so fast and by them investing at an early age. Time is on their side along with compounding interest and dividends. Being in your late 30's or 40's means that's planning for your retirement now is very important. People in their 50's and 60's should wake up and smell the roses or weeds, whatever they planted for themselves when they were young. Putting your saving in the buckets like mutual funds that have stocks, bonds, government securities is a good way to stay diversified in the changing word of finance. Owning your home is a big thing on my list for people everywhere young or old. Owning your home gives you extra money if you would need it by getting a first or second home equity loan. If you really want that feeling of independence start with the plan that I have been telling you about because actions and dreams are just words unless you start now.

Investment one - mutual funds in stocks, bonds government and corporate and ETF's

Investment two – real estate, residential and commercial

Emergency fund

Saving account

Cd's - certificate of deposits – some cd's are F.D.I.C insured

Life insurance - Life Insurance is not an investment it is a safety blanket that covers you when you die and provides for your family a pool upon your death. Be careful to only buy what you need at that time. If you have a family you may buy more without a family you buy less. Remember that term is cheaper when you are young but gets higher in cost as you get older. The whole life policy is a set amount that you set yourself. The whole life policy stays with you as long as you pay the premiums on it. Buying it at a young age saves you money then later you can add a term policy, if you need more insurance as your family grows.

Tip Bits

* Believe in yourself and the Lord will make good things happen.

* Life is full of peaks and valleys.

* Buy a silver dollar in the year your child or gran child was born so they can past it on to their children and tell them this was from your great gran mother and father. Later they can do the same for their children and gran children. The coin will turn into coins as it pasts down from family to family as each parent or gran parents buys coins for the new children born in the family.

* Have faith in God and yourself.

* It's not how much money you make it's what you do with it that counts.

* Read finance magazines, internet financial web sites, or listen to financial talk programs on business and investing. Read or listen to motivational books or speakers like Think and Grow Rich by author Napoleon Hill.

* Go to the bank and draw out $500.00 of $1.00 coins and put them in a fire proof or metal box. If there is ever a fire in your home the $500.00 coins will not burn. This little bit of money will help you and your family put gas

in the car, buy groceries and afford a place to spend the night until your insurance company helps you and your family the next day.

* I'm not cheap, I'm frugal so ask if it's a need or a want. A need is now, a want is later.

* Make copies of all your personal information and store it in a safe or metal box for safe keeping. Example copies of driver license, credit card numbers, medical records etc.

* Some people have rich man's taste and poor man's pockets. Be frugal in the things you buy.

* Matthew 25:14 – 14 is the parable of the talents or known as today parable of the bags of gold. God gives us all talents and we need to find them and use our talents. If we don't use our talents to help our self's and others to have a better life we will lose what we have.

Example: If you are giving a gift of a warm sweater and don't take in out of the box it can't keep you warm.

* Stocks – I put $25,000 into one blue chip company. This company was so big that I thought that it was too big to fail. That same company filed for bankruptcy leaving the people holding their shares of common stock with nothing but empty pockets. The same company reorganized itself under the federal government and

now is back in business with all new stock holders. The bottom line is that companies look after themselves for getting the people they ripped off to get where they are at. In the beginning start out in mutual funds, index funds or ETF's before you start buying individual stocks.

* LLC. – If you decide on gone in to business for yourself or with a partner think about setting up an LLC. (Limited Liability Corporation).

If you were to get sued they could not take away all your assets outside the LLC. Only the assets inside the LLC. You can start a new company up the following week under a new name under a new LLC. And you are back in business again.

* Poor man's patent – Put your ideas on paper and send it to yourself through the United States Postal service. Address the package or letter to yourself in a certified letter.

* Op money – Try to use op money when buying houses, stocks, investments etc. By using op money (other people's money) you free up your own money for when you really need it. Op money will be the money that comes from other sources such as banks or other money lenders. The money you borrow for your investments from the banks or money lenders may be considered a business transaction and in some cases the interest may be tax

deductible. The interest you pay on your mortgage or business loan may be tax deductible check with your tax accountant to be sure.

* Lending clubs – Lending clubs are sometimes a good source to earn better interest rates on your money than banks or certificates of deposit. One word of caution on lending clubs. Your money is not insured by the F.D.I.C and you may lose It. If you lose your money you may be able to deduct the loses from your income taxes as a business lost. Lending clubs are lending out your money to people as a promissory note with the agreement saying the person agrees to pay it back with a certain rate of interest in a certain number of months or years.

* Save time and money – Want a project done around your home. Call three contractors and get three estimates. Have them write down all the material parts and sizes of the material being used for the job. Request a starting and finishing date. Get a separate cost of per man – hour (uninterrupted labor). Go by all the material and after the job is completed, take the left over material not used back to the store and get your refund. Sometimes contractors over estimate the job and take the left over material to the next job site.

Rope of Life

In this world of rich and poor, there are dreams of life for ever more. There is an invisible rope of life that has no feelings nor respect, another life gone with no regrets. As a child he began climbing this rope of life. As a child so sweet and kind holding on to the rope of life with his little hand, hoping someday to climb to be a man. As each year turned he moved up one notch, now at the age of nine he has learned a lot. Learning to win victories over hunger and poor, he has built up power to survive some more. Now at the age of eighteen he goes into fight, for peace and love and what is right. Freedom is won only by war and he is glad he survived once more. Many notches he has climbed but knowing behind him is Father Time. Many notches he has climbed and even got married and settled down. He is older now and his muscles ache but remember to live will power it takes. Pray to be healthy and strong and to help other people where they may go wrong. It gets tougher each notch he climbs knowing there is an invisible rope of life that has no feelings nor respect. Hang in there and fight through all the blood and hell and you will survive very well.

By Joe Citrano Jr.

Life – Its not where you came from that counts its where you are gone that counts.

Glossary

Blue Collar – a working- class person better known as a blue collar worker because they wore blue uniforms and were paid hourly rates of pay and did manual labor.

Stocks – a type of security held in the ownership in a company and a share of their earnings and assets. Two types of stock – common and preferred.

LLC. – a limited liability company – is a business structure that combines the pass-through taxation of a partnership or sole proprietorship with the limited liability of a corporation.

Laddering – Joe's laddering in a technique of getting the equity out of one home to buy another and using it more than one time to buy more homes.

Mutual Fund – is an investment vehicle made up of a pool of funds collected from many investors for the purpose of investing in securities such as stocks, bonds, money markets instruments and similar assets.

ETF – Exchange Traded Fund – trades like a stock. a security that tracks the index. Carries a bucket of assets in it such as stocks and bonds.

Promissory Note – a signed document containing a written promise to pay a stated sum of money to a specified person or the bearer at a specified date or on demand.

Easement – the right to cross or other wise use someone else's land for a specified purpose.

Advisor – consultant, counselor, mentor, a person who gives you advice.

Diversification – a wide range of stocks, bonds real estate etc. in a portfolio that reduces the risk of you losing all your assets.

Dollar Cost Averaging – investing the same amount of money each month in a saving account or mutual fund.

Townhouse / Rowhome – a group of homes all connected tog

The Message

The years of 2008 and 2009 were bad for people like myself, but it taught me to be stronger and wiser with my money. Remember it's not how much money you make, it's what you do with it that counts. Over the years the economy turned around and people started to get back to work again. The investments in single stocks, mutual funds, ETF's, promissory notes and rental properties finally paid off. The times I spent in my younger days investing and taking chances have now giving me Financial Freedom in the Future. I still don't mind taking some chances on investments, but I have to be a little more careful. It's easy to lose money and it's sometimes hard to make it back. I hope you enjoyed reading about Financial Freedom in the Future and the peaks and valleys that life brings to all of us. Grow your assets over the years so you can enjoy a happy retirement. I hope you seek the courage, strength, wisdom and faith that I pray for every day. So, I may help others have a better understanding and purpose in life. Thank you and God Bless America.

Joe's spreadsheet for one of his properties

2018 PROPERTY RECORDS — 610 Cottenwood Drive

	CHECK NUMBER		DATE	AMOUNT	utilities	TAXES	insurance	RENT	MORT.	MAINT.	NOTES
6	DEBIT	INTERNET	1/2/2018	$20.00							
7	DEBIT	cellphone	1/2/2018	$20.00							
8	DEBIT	CRF	1/2/2018	$180.55							
9	ck. 001	waterbill	1/2/2018	$100.00	$100.00						
10	RENT	BB CORP.	1/2/2018	$1,000.00				$1,000.00			
11	ck. 002	MORT.	1/2/2018	$500.00					$500.00		
12											
13											
14	Debit	INTERNET	2/1/2018	$20.00							
15	DEBIT	cellphone	2/1/2018	$20.00							
16	DEBIT	CRF	2/1/2018	$180.55							
17	RENT	BB CORP.	2/1/2018	$1,000.00				$1,000.00			
18	CK. 003	waterbill	2/1/2018	$100.00	$100.00						
19	ck. 004	MORT.	2/1/2018	$500.00					$500.00		

Example of spreadsheet for each property you have.

This is a good way to keep records.

Residential Lease

Clause 1. Identification of Landlord and Tenant

This agreement is entered into between _____ [Tenant] and
_____ [Landlord]. Each Tenant is jointly and severally liable for the
payment of rent and performance of all other terms of this Agreement.

Clause 2. Identification of Premises

Subject to the terms and conditions in this Agreement, Landlord rents to Tenant, and Tenant rents from Landlord, for
residential purposes only, the premises located at _____
_____ together with the following furnishings and appliances:
_____ .

Rental of the premises also includes _____
_____ .

Clause 3. Limits on Use and Occupancy

The premises are to be used only as a private residence for Tenant(s) listed in Clause 1 of this Agreement, and their
minor children. Occupancy by guests for more than _____ is
prohibited without Landlord's written consent and will be considered a breach of this Agreement.

Clause 4. Term of the Tenancy

The rental will begin on _____, and end on _____ . If
Tenant vacates before the term ends, Tenant will be liable for the balance of the rent for the remainder of the term.

Clause 5. Payment of Rent.

Regular month rent

Tenant will pay to Landlord a monthly rent of $ _____ , payable in advance on the first day of each month,
except when that day falls on a weekend or legal holiday, in which case rent is due on the next business day. Rent will
be paid in the following manner unless Landlord designates otherwise:

Delivery of Payment.

Rent will be paid:

☐ by mail, to _____

☐ in person, at _____

Form of payment.

Landlord will accept payment in these forms:

☐ personal check made payable to _____

☐ cashier's check made payable to _____

☐ credit card

☐ money order

☐ cash

Prorated first month's rent.

For the period from Tenant's move-in date, _____ , through the end of the month, Tenant will pay to Landlord the prorated monthly rent of $ _____ . This amount will be paid on or before the date the Tenant moves in.

Clause 6. Late Charges

If Tenant fails to pay the rent in full before the end of the _____ day after it's due, Tenant will pay Landlord a late charge as follows: _____
_____ .

Landlord does not waive the right to insist on payment of the rent in full on the date it is due.

Clause 7. Returned Check and Other Bank Charges

If any check offered by Tenant to Landlord in payment of rent or any other amount due under this Agreement is returned for lack of sufficient funds, a "stop payment," or any other reason, Tenant will pay Landlord a returned check charge of $_____ .

Clause 8. Security Deposits

On signing this Agreement, Tenant will pay to Landlord the sum of $ _____ as a security deposit. Tenant may not, without Landlord's prior written consent, apply this security deposit to the last month's rent or to any other sum due under this Agreement. Within _____ after Tenant has vacated the premises, returned keys, and provided Landlord with a forwarding address, Landlord will return the deposit in full or give Tenant an itemized written statement of the reasons for, and the dollar amount of, any of the security deposit retained by Landlord, along with a check for any deposit balance.

Clause 9. Utilities

Tenant will pay all utility charges, except for the following, which will be paid by Landlord:
_____
_____

Clause 10. Assignment and Subletting

Tenant will not sublet any part of the premises or assign this Agreement without the prior written consent of Landlord.

Clause 11. Tenant's Maintenance Responsibilities

Tenant will: (1) keep the premises clean, sanitary, and in good condition and, upon termination of the tenancy, return the premises to Landlord in a condition identical to that which existed when Tenant took occupancy, except for ordinary wear and tear; (2) immediately notify Landlord of any defects or dangerous conditions in and about the premises of which Tenant becomes aware; and (3) reimburse Landlord, on demand by Landlord, for the cost of any repairs to the premises damaged by Tenant or Tenant's guests or business invitees through misuse or neglect.

Tenant has examined the premises, including appliances, fixtures, carpets, drapes, and paint, and has found them to be in good, safe, and clean condition and repair, except as noted in the Landlord-Tenant Checklist.

Clause 12. Repairs and Alterations by Tenant

a. Except as provided by law, or as authorized by the prior written consent of Landlord, Tenant will not make any repairs or alterations to the premises, including nailing holes in the walls or painting the rental unit.

b. Tenant will not, without Landlord's prior written consent, alter, rekey, or install any locks to the premises or install or alter any burglar alarm system. Tenant will provide Landlord with a key or keys capable of unlocking all such rekeyed or new locks as well as instructions on how to disarm any altered or new burglar alarm system.

Clause 13. Violating Laws and Causing Disturbances

Tenant is entitled to quiet enjoyment of the premises. Tenant and guests or invitees will not use the premises or adjacent areas in such a way as to: (1) violate any law or ordinance, including laws prohibiting the use, possession, or sale of illegal drugs; (2) commit waste (severe property damage); or (3) create a nuisance by annoying, disturbing, inconveniencing, or interfering with the quiet enjoyment and peace and quiet of any other tenant or nearby resident.

Clause 14. Pets

No animal, bird, or other pet will be kept on the premises, even temporarily, except properly trained service animals needed by blind, deaf, or disabled persons and _____ under the following conditions:

_____

_____

_____ .

Clause 15. Landlord's Right to Access

Landlord or Landlord's agents may enter the premises in the event of an emergency, to make repairs or improvements, or to show the premises to prospective buyers or tenants. Landlord may also enter the premises to conduct an annual inspection to check for safety or maintenance problems. Except in cases of emergency, Tenant's abandonment of the premises, court order, or where it is impractical to do so, Landlord shall give Tenant _____ notice before entering.

Clause 16. Extended Absences by Tenant

Tenant will notify Landlord in advance if Tenant will be away from the premises for _____ or more consecutive days. During such absence, Landlord may enter the premises at times reasonably necessary to maintain the property and inspect for needed repairs.

Clause 17. Possession of the Premises

    a.   *Tenant's failure to take possession.*

        If, after signing this Agreement, Tenant fails to take possession of the premises, Tenant will still be responsible for paying rent and complying with all other terms of this Agreement.

    b.   *Landlord's failure to deliver possession.*

        If Landlord is unable to deliver possession of the premises to Tenant for any reason not within Landlord's control, including, but not limited to, partial or complete destruction of the premises, Tenant will have the right to terminate this Agreement upon proper notice as required by law. In such event, Landlord's liability to Tenant will be limited to the return of all sums previously paid by Tenant to Landlord.

Clause 18. Tenant Rules and Regulations

    ☐ Tenant acknowledges receipt of, and has read a copy of, tenant rules and regulations, which are attached to and incorporated into this Agreement by this reference.

Clause 19. Payment of Court Costs and Attorney Fees in a Lawsuit

In any action or legal proceeding to enforce any part of this Agreement, the prevailing party
☐ shall not / ☐ shall recover reasonable attorney fees and court costs.

Clause 20. Disclosures

Tenant acknowledges that Landlord has made the following disclosures regarding the premises:

    ☐ Disclosure of Information on Lead-Based Paint and/or Lead-Based Paint Hazards

    ☐ Other disclosures:

Clause 21. Authority to Receive Legal Papers

The Landlord, any person managing the premises, and anyone designated by the Landlord are authorized to accept service of process and receive other notices and demands, which may be delivered to:

☐ The Landlord, at the following address: _____ .
☐ The manager, at the following address: _____ .
☐ The following person, at the following address: _____

_____

Clause 22. Additional Provisions

Additional provisions are as follows:

_____
_____
_____
_____

Clause 23. Validity of Each Part

If any portion of this Agreement is held to be invalid, its invalidity will not affect the validity or enforceability of any other provision of this Agreement.

Clause 24. Grounds for Termination of Tenancy

The failure of Tenant or Tenant's guests or invitees to comply with any term of this Agreement, or the misrepresentation of any material fact on Tenant's rental application, is grounds for termination of the tenancy, with appropriate notice to Tenant and procedures as required by law.

Clause 25. Entire Agreement

This document constitutes the entire Agreement between the parties, and no promises or representations, other than those contained here and those implied by law, have been made by Landlord or Tenant. Any modifications to this Agreement must be in writing signed by Landlord and Tenant.

_____   _____   _____
Date   Landlord or Landlord's Agent   Title

_____
Address

_____   _____   _____   _____
City   State   Zip Code   Phone

_____   _____   _____
Date   Tenant   Phone

_____   _____   _____
Date   Tenant   Phone

_____   _____   _____
Date   Tenant   Phone

Disclosure of Information on Lead-Based Paint and/or Lead-Based Paint Hazards

Lead Warning Statement

Housing built before 1978 may contain lead-based paint. Lead from paint, paint chips, and dust can pose health hazards if not managed properly. Lead exposure is especially harmful to young children and pregnant women. Before renting pre-1978 housing, lessors must disclose the presence of known lead-based paint and/or lead-based paint hazards in the dwelling. Lessees must also receive a federally approved pamphlet on lead poisoning prevention.

Lessor's Disclosure

(a) Presence of lead-based paint and/or lead-based paint hazards (check (i) or (ii) below):

    (i) _____ Known lead-based paint and/or lead-based paint hazards are present in the housing (explain).

    _____

    _____

    (ii) _____ Lessor has no knowledge of lead-based paint and/or lead-based paint hazards in the housing.

(b) Records and reports available to the lessor (check (i) or (ii) below):

    (i) _____ Lessor has provided the lessee with all available records and reports pertaining to lead-based paint and/or lead-based paint hazards in the housing (list documents below).

    _____

    _____

    (ii) _____ Lessor has no reports or records pertaining to lead-based paint and/or lead-based paint hazards in the housing.

Lessee's Acknowledgment (initial)

(c) _____ Lessee has received copies of all information listed above.

(d) _____ Lessee has received the pamphlet _Protect Your Family from Lead in Your Home._

Agent's Acknowledgment (initial)

(e) _____ Agent has informed the lessor of the lessor's obligations under 42 U.S.C. 4852d and is aware of his/her responsibility to ensure compliance.

Certification of Accuracy

The following parties have reviewed the information above and certify, to the best of their knowledge, that the information they have provided is true and accurate.

Lessor	Date	Lessor	Date
Lessee	Date	Lessee	Date
Agent	Date	Agent	Date

LEASE AGREEMENT FOR COMMERCIAL PROPERTIES

(This lease agreement is a legally binding contract; if not understood, seek competent advice before signing.)

THIS DEED OF LEASE, made this _____ day of_____, _____, by and between TENANT_____, hereinafter referred to as "Tenant", and LANDLORD, JOSEPH CINTRA, hereinafter referred to as "Landlord".

WITNESSETH:

1. Address of Property Term/Rent:

THAT IN CONSIDERATION of the premises rents and covenants herein expressed, Landlord hereby leases to Tenant and Tenants rents form Landlord, upon the terms and conditions herein forth, the certain unfurnished property known as _____ Baltimore, Maryland, ("the property") for the term commencing on the _____ day of _____, and ending on the _____ day of _____, _____, for the total sum during the term.

_____has agreed to lease the property known as _____FROM Joseph Cintra. – LANDLORD at and for the following rents:

	Date/Year		Date/Year		Per Month Rent
First Year	_____	thru	_____	=	_____
Second Year	_____	thru	_____	=	_____
Third Year	_____	thru	_____	=	_____
Fourth Year	_____	thru	_____	=	_____
Fifth Year	_____	thru	_____	=	_____

2. Payments:

Rent shall be payable to Landlord as identified at the address as follows: Joseph Cintra, Jr., 5366 Cottenwood Drive, Baltimore, MD 1111. Phone Number: xxx-xxx-xxxx Cell-xxx-xxx-xxxx. If rent is sent to any other address or location than above, paragraph 3 may apply.

3. Late Fee Cost of Returned Checks:

If any installment of rent is not received by the Landlord within five days from the due date, Tenant covenants and agrees to pay as additional rent five percent (5%) of the unpaid rent. Tenant further agrees to pay a handling charge of $35.00 for each check returned by the bank for insufficient funds or any other reason. Landlord may require any and all payments to be made in cash, money order or certified funds.

4. Good Repair:

Landlord will lease the property to tenant in good working order and Tenant shall return the property to Seller at the end of the Lease Agreement in a clean condition and with all fixtures and equipment in good working order. Repairs or replacement of equipment provided due to normal wear and tear shall be at the expense of the Tenant. Tenants will be responsible for maintenance and warranty of heating and air conditioning equipment. Tenants will be billed for the maintenance policy covering heating and air conditioning equipment. If any property repairs are required Tenants must use licensed contractors to perform repairs. Landlord must be contacted prior to repairs to approve contractor. Tenants are responsible for all repairs for interior and exterior of the building including roof. Tenants are responsible for general maintenance and storefront glass as stated in covenant 15 of this lease.

5. Locks:

The cost for changing locks upon tenant vacating premises shall be deducted from the security deposit.

6. Security Deposit:

Tenant has deposited with the Landlord on _____ the sum of _____, which sum does not exceed two months rent, which is to be held as a security deposit and applied to any rent or unpaid water bills that may remain due and owing at the expiration of the agreement, any extension thereof or holding over period applied to any damages to the premises caused by the Tenant, his family, guests, employees, trades people or other damages suffered by Landlord as a result of a branch of covenant or provisions of this lease. Landlord will not pay interest on the security deposit. All final utility bills must be paid in full, and Tenant must provide a receipt for last water bill. Tenant may not utilize the security deposit as rent and he shall not apply the same as the last month's rent. In the event that any part of the said security deposit shall have been utilized by Landlord on behalf of Landlord in accordance with the term hereof or applicable law, the Tenant, shall, upon delivery of same, immediately deposit with the Agent the amount so applied by Landlord so that Landlord shall have the full deposit on hand at all times during the term of this lease or any renewal thereof or holding over. Upon written request from Tenant, Landlord shall promptly provide Tenant with a written list of all damages. Said request must be made within fifteen (15) days of the Tenant's occupancy. The Landlord shall provide the Tenant, within thirty (30) days after the end of the tenancy, by first class mail directed to the last known address of the tenant, a written list of all damages to premises together with a statement of costs actually incurred. Within (30) days after the end of the tenancy, the Landlord shall return the deposit to the Tenant, from a non-interest bearing account, less any damages rightfully withheld. Repairs required may be so substantial or of such a nature that work will not be completed within the thirty (30) day period following the termination to the tenancy, in which case tenant shall be notified of projected or estimated costs by an itemized list of damages, to be followed by a statement to Tenant costs actually spent by Landlord, as soon as Landlord is apprised of such information. Tenant has the right to be present at time of inspection to determine if any damage has been done to the premises if Tenant notifies Landlord by certified mail fifteen (15) days prior to Tenant's intention to move, his date of moving and new address. Upon receipt of notice, Landlord shall notify Tenant by certified mail of time and date when premises are to be inspected. The inspection date shall occur within five (5) days after date of moving as designated in Tenant's notice.

7. Possession of Premises:

In the event that Landlord is unable to deliver possession of the premises at the commencement of the tenancy, the Landlord agrees to use whatever efforts are, in his determination, reasonable to secure possession of the premises for Tenant, including recovery of possession against a for occupant wrongfully holding over, but in no event, except of the willful and deliberate misconduct of Landlord be liable to tenant for any delay in possession. Not withstanding the provisions of the foregoing sentence. Tenant shall have no responsibility to rent for the time elapsing from the beginning of the term of this lease until the premises are available for occupancy of Tenant.

8. Condition of Properties:

Tenant has made an initial inspection of the property, and Tenant agrees that the property is in a fit condition, except for such damages or malfunctions as shall be itemized in writing on a record made by Tenant or Landlord. A copy of such record shall be retained by Tenant and Landlord. Any additional items to be noted should be received by Landlord within fifteen (15) day of occupancy, in writing, to be determined as legitimate, and added, if required.

9. Default of Rent:

In the event that Tenant fails to pay when due any installment of rent, or additional rent, such rent, or additional rent, is not paid within five (5) days after written notice by Landlord of non-payment and of intention to terminate this lease, in addition to other remedies provided by law, Landlord may terminate this lease. Upon such termination, Landlord shall be entitled to possession of the property, to any unpaid rent or additional rent, to recover any damages sustained and to such attorney's fees as may be recoverable by law. It is further covenanted and agreed between the parties hereto that is any installment of rent hereinbefore reserved not paid at the time and place agreed upon, although no formal or legal demand shall have been made for the same, or if any of the covenants, conditions, or agreements herein contained shall not be performed or observed by the Tenant, according to their full tenor and effort, or in case the leased premises shall be deserted or vacated, then in either or any of said events the Landlord may proceed to recover possession of said premises in accordance with the law governing proceedings between Landlord and Tenant.

All payments, charges and expenses required to be paid by the Tenant under any of the provisions of this Lease, over and above the rent reserved herein, including but not limited to operating expenses, shall be deemed to be Additional Rent (whether characterized as such in this Lease or not) and in the event of non-payment, Landlord shall be entitled to pursue all remedies, at Law or in Equity, for their collection as rent in arrears including the right of distraint.

In the event of Tenant default or bankruptcy, a Promissory Note under this Agreement between the Tenant(s) and Landlord will supersede this lease and all terms and agreements herein. All monies owed under the original terms of this lease will become the responsibility and obligation of Tenants as individuals and guaranteed to be paid in full to Landlord under terms of Promissory Note.

10. Transfer of Security Deposit:

The property is managed by the Landlord. Should the management transfer to any other party by contract, the Tenant consents to the transfer of his security deposit to such party, if applicable.

11. Attorney's Fee and Enforcement:

Tenant further covenants and agrees that in the event of his default in any installment of rent, or in the event of his breach of any covenant or condition hereof, that he will reimburse the Landlord for any money expended by Landlord for utility or other bill, damages, relating costs, as well as other costs which may be incurred to enforce this lease, such as reasonable attorney's fees being 20% of any sums owed to Landlord by Tenant.

12. Plumbing and Appliances:

Tenant will keep the premises, including all plumbing fixtures, facilities, and air conditioning and heating equipment as clean and safe as condition permits and shall unstop and keep clear all waste pipes, drains and water closets thereon. The Tenant expressly covenants and agrees that at the termination of the lease, all equipment will be in good working order shall be operative and that the premises will be in good, clean condition, ordinary wear and tear expected. All utility services shall be ordered disconnected and all final bills paid by Tenant before any part of the security deposit can be returned. The Tenant is responsible for loss or damage from freezing of water pipes or plumbing fixtures or from stopping of water closets and drains, which shall be repaired at the expense of the Tenant.

13. Use and Repair of Facilities:

Tenant will use in a reasonable manner all electrical, plumbing, sanitary, heating, ventilating, air conditioning, and other fixtures, facilities and appliances in the premises, and Tenant shall be responsible to repair them at his expense for any damage caused by his failure to comply with this requirement.

14. Damaging Property:

Tenant will not deliberately or negligently destroy, deface, damage, impair, or remove any part of the premises (including fixtures, facilities and equipment) or permit any person to do so whether known by the Tenant or not, and Tenant shall be responsible for any damage caused by his failure to comply with this requirement. Tenant shall promptly remove ice and/or snow as necessary and/or required by local ordinance.

15. General Maintenance:

Tenant will, at his own expense:

A. Keep in good condition any walks in good repair, natural wear and tear expected.

B. Remove leaves and other debris that accumulates on the property.

C. Promptly remove ice and snow as necessary and/ or required by local ordinance.

D. Keep gutters, downspouts and exterior drains clear of any leaves and other debris.

E. Furnish his own light bulbs, furnace filters and fuses.

F. Replace or repair all broken or damaged glass, screens, roof, ceiling tiles, flooring, and drywall occurring during his tenancy.

G. Keep property in a good states of cleanliness, including equipment, and keep property free from objectionable features, nuisances and hazards.

H. Keep grass cut short and all weeds pulled for neat and clean appearance.

I. Dispose of own trash if no pick up by City or County. Landlord may require a dumpster at Tenants expense.

J. Any repair or replacement of property, equipment or appliances necessary due to the negligence by acts of commission or omission of Tenant, of his guests, shall be paid by the Tenant. Tenant will not place any heavy articles in property without the written consent of Landlord.

K. It is the responsibility of the tenant to contact the Local Merchant's Association to obtain a copy of the by laws and governing their area and to abide by these restrictions. Failure to do so could result in fines or penalties which will be the sole responsibility of the tenant and will be a direct violation of this contract.

L. Tenant pays for heating/air conditioning and hot water heater maintenance policy.

M. Tenants are responsible for all building maintenance both interior and exterior including the roof.

N. Tenant shall show proof of insurance on business going into property.

O. Tenant shall not have any open flame in the building.

16. Notice of Defects or Malfunctions:

Landlord has the right to inspect the property as, if and when repairs are needed. Tenant will give Landlord prompt notice of any defects or malfunctions during the Lease. Tenant is responsible to pay for any repairs or replacements.

17. Tenant Conduct:

Tenant shall conduct himself and require other persons on the premises whether known by the Tenant or not, to conduct themselves in a manner that will not disturb his neighbors' peaceful enjoyment of their premises, and the Tenant further covenants and agrees that he will not use nor permit said premises to be used for any improper, illegal, or immoral purposes, nor will he use, permit or suffer same to be used by any person or persons in any noisy, dangerous, offensive, illegal, or improper manner.

18. Health and Safety:

Tenants shall comply with all obligations primarily imposed upon tenants by applicable provisions of building and housing codes materially affecting health and safety.

19. Equipment That Overloads a System:

Tenant will not install or use, or permit to be installed or used, any equipment of any kind that will require any alterations or additions to, or create and overload on, any gas, water, heating, electrical, sewerage, draining, or air conditioning systems of the said property without prior written consent of the Landlord, and the permission of any governmental

agency or public utility company, as and if required, and compliance with applicable public laws.

20. Explosives and Inflammables:

The Tenant will not use or keep on the property any explosives, or inflammable or combustible materials, which would increase the rate of fire insurance on the premises.

21. Smoke Detectors:

If any applicable law of any governmental body requires the installation of Smoke Detectors at the time of occupancy of the leased premises by Tenant, Landlord certifies to Tenant that said Smoke Detectors have been installed and is in proper working condition in accordance with said law prior to Tenant's occupancy. It shall be the responsibility of Tenant to check working condition and to report the malfunction of said Smoke Detectors to Landlord in writing. Landlord assumes no responsibility or liability for any non-reported malfunction to or misuse of Smoke Detectors by the Tenant which results in injury or damage to the leased premises. It shall be the responsibility of the Tenant to obtain an insurance policy, which provides liability coverage and also provides for the protection of Tenant's personal property.

22. Redecorating and Alterations:

Tenant shall obtain written permission before redecorating and shall not make any alterations, additions, or improvements without first obtaining Landlord's written consent. Such alterations, etc. shall, at the option of Landlord, remain with the property or be removed by tenant and premises returned to original condition at the expense of the Tenant.

23. Trash Removal:

Tenant shall provide appropriate receptacles for the condition; storage and removal of garbage, rubbish, and other waste and arrange for the removal of same.

24. Utility, Charges, Dues, and Fees:

Tenant will pay all utility charges, including but not limited to gas, water, sewer fee-per real property tax bill, electricity, waste removal and telephone. Said utility charges will commence on the effective day of this lease. Tenant agrees he will pay the bills promptly when due and will make all necessary deposits as quoted by utility companies. All utility services shall be ordered disconnected and all final bills paid by tenant, with proof of receipts, before any part of the security deposit can be returned. Landlord shall not be liable, in any manner, for failure, interruption, or stoppage of gas, electricity and/ or water at any time.

25. Notice of Absence:

Tenant shall give Landlord notice of an anticipated extended absence of Tenant from property in excess of seven (7) days. During any such absence of Tenant, Landlord may enter the property at any time reasonably necessary to protect the property and possession of Landlord on or in the property.

26. Subordination and Assignment of Lease:

This lease shall be subordinate to the lien of existing and future mortgages placed on the premises, and Tenant agrees to execute whatever additional agreements are required to so subordinate this lease. Landlord shall have the right to assign any of his rights under this Agreement at any time.

27. Access to Property by Landlord, Agent and Their DulyDesignated Representatives:

Upon reasonable notice to Tenant and at reasonable times, Landlord, or his duly designated representatives, may enter the premises in order to:

A. Inspect the property;

B. Make necessary repairs, decorations, alterations, or improvements;

C. Supply necessary or agreed services;

D. Exhibit the property to prospective or actual purchasers or tenants, mortgagers, appraisers, workmen or other contractors, and;

5. In addition, sixty (60) days preceding the expiration or termination of said term, Tenant will allow a "for rent" or a "for sale" sign to be placed on the property, along with a lockbox containing a key to the main entrance for prospective tenants' and purchasers; access.

28. Tenants Refusal to Allow Access:

If Tenant refuses to allow access to Landlord or his designated representatives as provided in preceding Paragraph 28, Landlord may obtain injunctive relief to compel access or may terminate this lease. If Tenant fails to vacate the property, Landlord may bring action for possession and damages sustained, including re-letting costs and reasonable attorney's fees. After termination of this lease, whether by expiration of the term or by termination by Landlord upon breach by Tenant, the property shall be promptly vacated, all personal property of Tenant shall be removed, property left in good and clean order by Tenant, reasonable wear and tear expected, utilities disconnected, and all final bills paid and proof of receipts provided.

29. Rights of Landlord Upon Breach of Lease by Tenant:

If Tenant violates any of the provisions this lease or any of the rules and regulations imposed by Landlord, or if any bankruptcy or insolvency proceedings are filed by or against Tenant (or a receiver or trustee is appointed for his property), or if the premises are vacated or abandoned, Landlord shall be entitled to avail himself of all rights and remedies to which he may be entitled either by law or in equity (including but not limited to the right to terminate this lease and recover possession and Landlord shall be also entitled to recover reasonable attorney's fees and costs as allowed by law. Landlord's waiver of one default by Tenant shall not be considered to be a waiver of any subsequent default. Tenant waives the benefits of any exemption under the homestead, bankruptcy, and any other insolvency law as to his obligation in this lease.

30. Truthfulness of Rental Application:

The Rental Application submitted by Tenant has been an inducement for Landlord to rent the premises to tenant. If any material facts in the Rental Application are untrue or if the premises are occupied by anyone other than

Tenant as stated in the Rental Application, Landlord shall have the right to terminate this lease to hold Tenant liable for any damage to the premises to avail himself of all rights and remedies to which he may be entitled at law or equity, and to recover reasonable attorney's fees and costs as allowed by law.

31. Liens Upon Property:

The Tenant has no authority to incur any debt or make any charge against the Landlord or create any lien upon the said leased property for any work, utilities or materials furnished to same.

32. Destruction by Casualty:

If the property shall be partially damaged by fire, rain, wind, or other cause, without the fault and neglect by Tenant, the damage shall be repaired within a reasonable time by and at the expense of Landlord and the rent, according to the extent that the property is damaged by fire or other cause, to such extent that Landlord shall decide not to restore the property to the former condition or Landlord shall decide to demolish the structures on said property, then and in either of such events, Landlord shall have the option to terminate this lease by written notice to Tenant, and the term of this lease shall terminate on the day such notice is given, with the balance of the rent due hereunder adjusted to the date of such termination.

33. Waiver of Breach:

No waiver or oversight of any breach of any covenants, conditions, or agreement herein contained, or compromised or settlement relating to such a breach, shall operate as a waiver of the covenant, condition or agreement itself, or any subsequent breach thereof.

34. Property Unfit for Occupancy:

If the whole, or any part, of said property should be declared, posted, or be the subject of formal notice, by or pursuant to any governmental authority or law, that it is unfit, unsafe, unsuitable, or not lawfully usable for the purpose or persons under this Lease, landlord shall have the option of eliminating or correcting the cause thereof, if such can be done, and Landlord elects to do so, or terminating this Lease from the date Landlord gives notice to Tenant of such termination or from the date Landlord is compelled by law to terminate further occupancy or use of said property, whichever date is earlier, and the remaining rent due hereunder shall be proportionately adjusted to the effective date of such termination.

35. Condemnation:

If the whole or any part of said property shall be taken or condemned pursuant to any governmental authority for any public or quasi-public use or purpose, the term of this Lease shall cease and terminate from the date when the possession of the part so taken or condemned shall be required for such use or purpose, and the remaining rent due hereunder shall be proportionately adjusted to the effective date of such termination.

36. Landlord Without Liability:

In no event shall Landlord or leasing agent be liable for damages or compensation to Tenant or Tenant's assigns, agents, or licensees, or other persons or entities, because of the events, conditions, actions or termination described in or arising from or connected with the provisions of Paragraph34.

37. Failure to Fulfill Covenants:

It is specifically covenanted and agreed between the parties here to that these presents are executed upon each and all of the conditions, covenants and agreements contained herein, and that if the Tenant, of his executors, administrators, or invitees, do or shall neglect, fail or refuse to perform or observe any covenants, conditions, agreements, or undertakings herein contained, or if said premises shall be deserted or vacated, then and in any said cases, in addition to other remedies therefore provided by law, the Landlord or those having estate in said premises, may lawfully for with or of any time thereafter, enter into and upon the said premises, or any part thereof, by fore or otherwise and without being liable for any prosecution, suit or damages thereto, and responses the same and expel the tenant for those claiming under or through him and remove his or their effect without demand or notice and without prejudice to any remedies which might otherwise be used for arrears of rent, or preceding breach of covenant, and this Lease shall terminate and end, and the Tenant hereby specifically agrees that he will indemnify the Landlord, its successors or assigns, against all loss or deficiency of rent or other payments which he may incur by reason of such termination and without further notice or consent of the Tenant may proceed to re-let such premises. The Tenant also agrees that all property on the said premises and for thirty (30) days after removal shall be liable to distress for said rent or on judgment obtained in a suit therefore.

38. Tenant Neglect and Costs:

If at any time during the term of this Lease, or any renewal or extension thereof, Landlord should be required by any governmental authority to make repairs, alterations or additions to said property or its equipment caused by the use or neglect thereof by Tenant, Tenant hereby agrees to have said repairs, alterations, or additions made at tenant's risk, cost and expense, and if Tenant fails to do so promptly, Landlord shall the option of terminating this

Lease, or causing such repairs, alterations, or additions to be made, and the cost of same, plus six percent (6%) interest thereof, shall be considered as additional rent for said property and payable forthwith by Tenant. The provisions of this paragraph shall be in addition to and shall not prevent the enforcement of any claim Landlord may have against Tenant for any other breach or damages under this Lease.

39. Unenforceable Clauses:

All individual provisions, paragraphs, sentences, clauses, sections and words in this lease shall be sever able and if any one or more such provisions, sections, paragraphs, sentences, clauses or words is determined by any court, administrative body, or tribunal, having proper jurisdiction, to be in any way enforceable, or to be in any way a violation of or in conflict with any law of any applicable jurisdiction such determination shall have no effect whatsoever on any of the remaining paragraphs, provisions, clauses, sections, sentences, or words of this Lease.

40. Liability for Personal or Property Damage:

All persons and personal property in or on said property shall be at the sole risk and responsibility of Tenant. Landlord shall not be liable for any damage or injury to said persons or personal property arising from the negligence, acts or omission of acts of any persons or entity, or from roof, wall, floor, door to window leaks, or from the freezing, bursting, leaking or overflowing of waste, stream, sewer, or gas pipes, or from heating or plumbing fixtures, or from electric wires or fixtures, or by any other cause whatsoever, latent or patent. In summary Landlord shall not be liable for any injury or damage whatsoever to the person or property of Tenant or any other person or entity in or on said property, and Tenant hereby expressly and without reservations covenants and agrees to save Landlord harmless in all such matters, unless such injury or damage is committed deliberately and with malice by Landlord.

41. WAIVER OF JURY TRIAL:

Landlord and Tenant hereby mutually waive any and all rights which either may have to request a jury trial in any action, proceeding or counterclaim (except for those involving personal injury or property damages) arising out of this Lease or Tenant's occupancy of or right to occupy the Leased Premises in any court of competent jurisdiction.

42. Pest Control:

Keep property clear and free of rodents and pests at Tenants expense.

43. Parking Agreement:

Parking agreement to lease parking space. Agreement for parking at 11 Eastern Drive. Signed parking agreement will be added to the lease agreement for _____Eastern Drive. One parking space for () years at ($50.00) fifty dollars per month added to the rent total amount.

THIS AGREEMENT is the entire agreement between the parties, and no modification or addition to it shall be binding unless signed by the parties hereto.

The covenants, conditions and agreements contained herein are binding upon and shall inure to the benefit of the parties hereto and their respective heirs, executors, administrators, personal representatives, successors and assigns. Tenants signing this Agreement shall be jointly and severally liable. Whatever the context so requires, the singular member shall include the plural, and the plural the singular, and the use of any gender shall include all genders.

_____is not acting as property manager for this property, but has acted only as the agent in locating a tenant for the Landlord. _____has no responsibility or liability for property management.

WITNESS THE FOLLOWING SIGNATURES AND SEALS:

_____

DATE   TENANT   (SEAL)

_____

DATE   TENANT   (SEAL)

_____

DATE   TENANT   (SEAL)

_____

DATE   TENANT   (SEAL)

_____

DATE   TENANT   (SEAL)

_____

DATE   TENANT   (SEAL)

_____LEASING FIRM BY:

_____(SEAL)

(Representative Agent)

SECURITY DEPOSIT RECEIVED: $ _____

FROM: _____

Notes

Notes

Notes

Notes

Notes

About the Author

Brandon Max was born and raised in Baltimore, MD in a community called Canton. He graduated from the Baltimore Public School System. Although he is not certificated as a realtor, financial planner, or stock broker, all the topics discussed in his book were learned through his lifetime experiences in managing his own businesses and working as a blue-collar worker, such as, warehouse, factory, and security jobs. He is writing this book to provide guidance to others so that they may avoid the mistakes he made and for them to go forward so they may have financial freedom in the future.

www.ingramcontent.com/pod-product-compliance
Lightning Source LLC
Chambersburg PA
CBHW030009190526
45157CB00014B/1394